RETRO
coloring books
.com

Retro Glamping
Coloring Book for Grown-Ups
Volume 1
by Karen Douglas

Retro Glamping Coloring Book for Grown-ups, Volume 1
Copyright ©2016 Karen Douglas

Printed in the United States of America

First Printing, 2016   ISBN-13: 978-0692601037, ISBN-10: 0692601031

Retro Coloring Books
P.O. Box 725
Oak Grove, MO 64075

www.retrocoloringbooks.com

The images of the travel trailers were created by the traditional method of using pencil to sketch and then using pen to ink in the lines. Then they were scanned in, cleaned up, and vector graphics were created. They are an expression of my love of all things retro and especially my love of campers and restoring or glamping them. These illustrations are meant to be reminiscent of the coloring book pages we would have seen as children. They are left to your imagination to fill in with wonderful colors, flowers, and patterns. Please color outside the lines, use dots and stripes, or whatever you can imagine ... I'd love to see them when you are finished; just use the hash tag #retrocoloringbooks on Instagram and Twitter or join our Facebook page!

The drawings which follow each trailer illustration were created in Adobe Illustrator to take advantage of what technology does well, which is to create repeating patterns. Because we all know how much fun those are to color, I couldn't leave them out! Each illustration was inspired by the camper on the preceding page. In this example, the trees inspired thoughts of the north and with that the warm coziness of a Nordic sweater. I hope you enjoy coloring these in as much as I did drawing them.

A quick sampling of pages

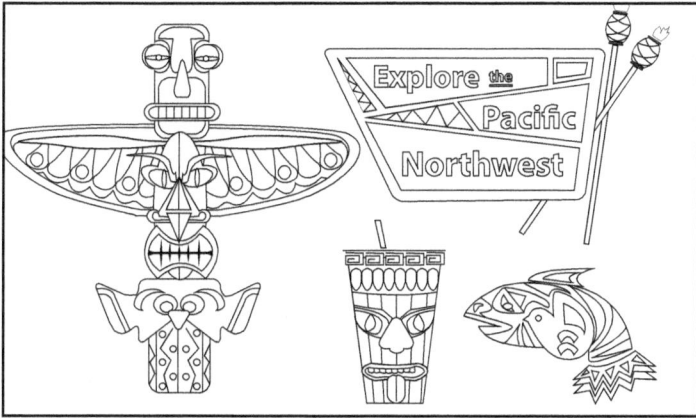

Feel free to use colored pencils, markers, or a variety of other media to color in this book. To help prevent bleed-thru, you may want to place a blank sheet of paper between the pages when coloring.

Each of the pages are intentionally left blank on the back side so that you don't have to worry about bleed-thru ruining the next image and to make it more convenient for removal and display. They are printed so that you turn the book sideways and view the page horizontally, this should make coloring them easier and more enjoyable for you.

Use this space to sketch your own camper.

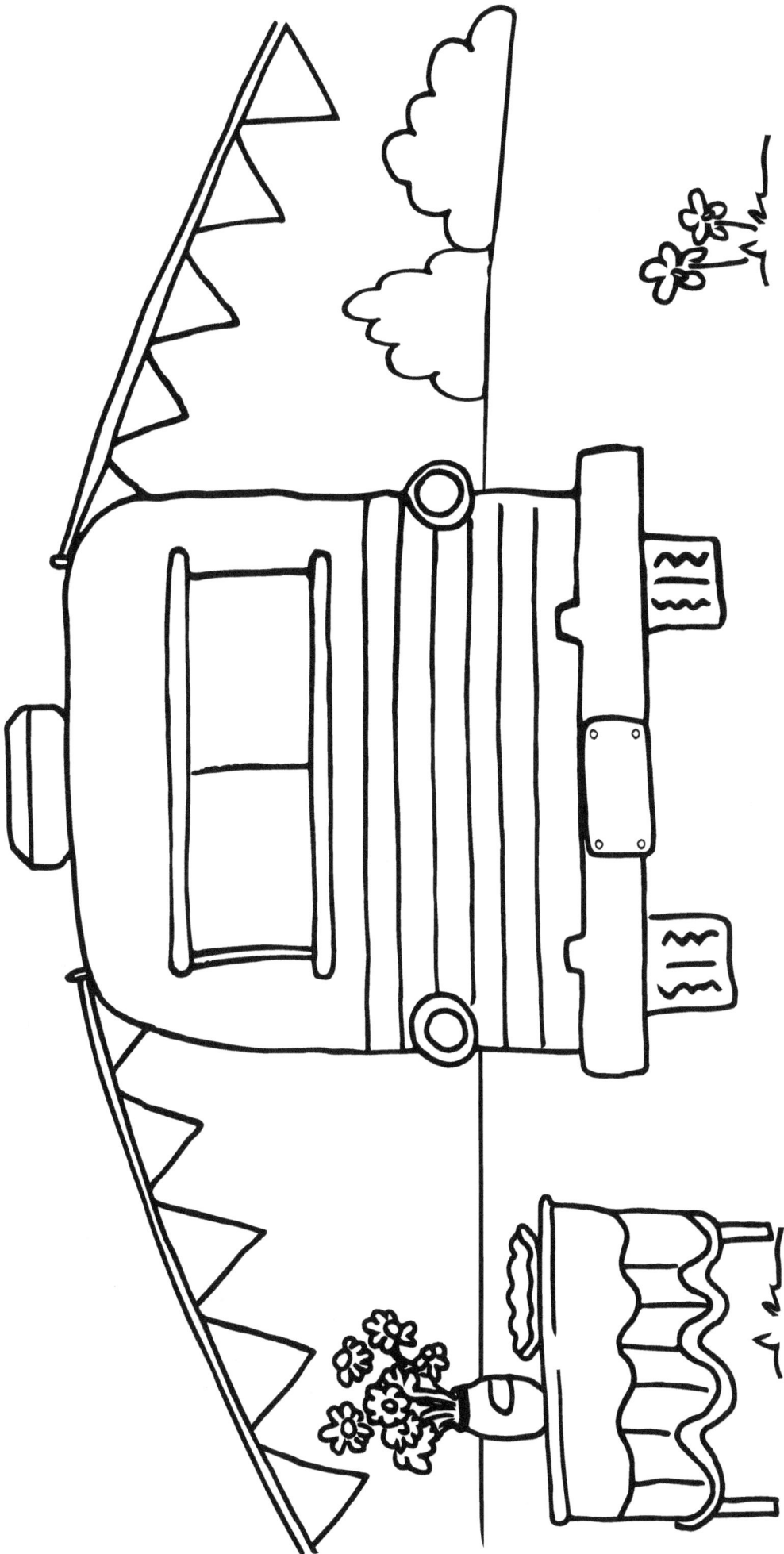

Hello
my name is:

Happy Glamper

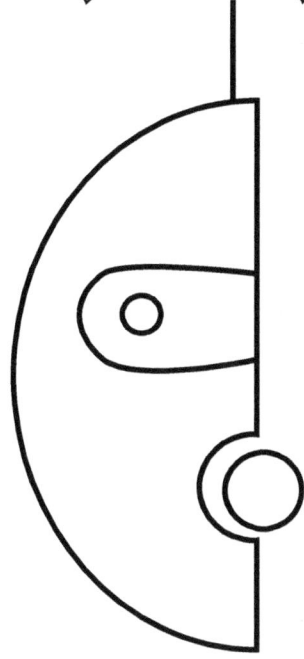

Relaxing at the beach

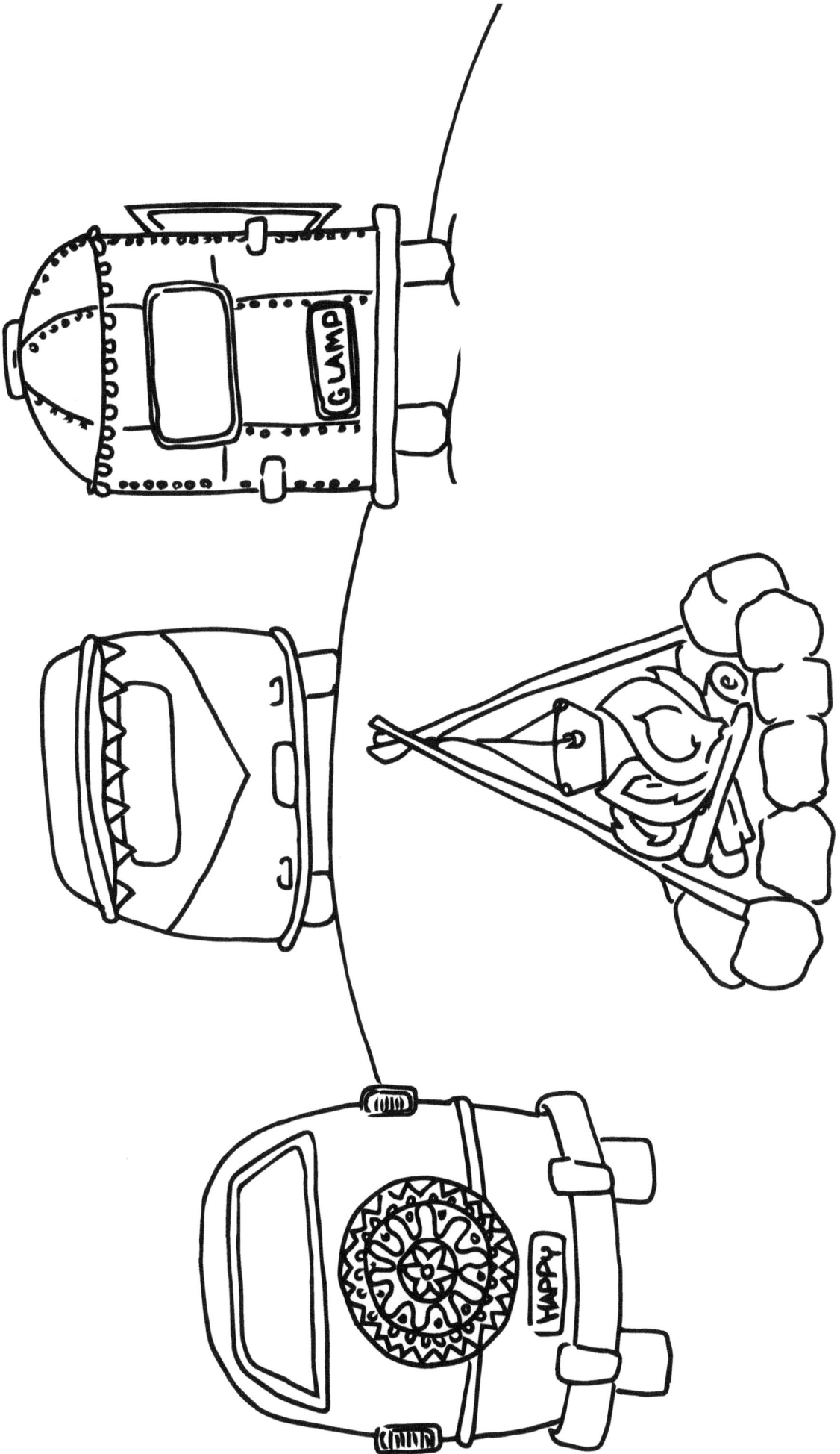

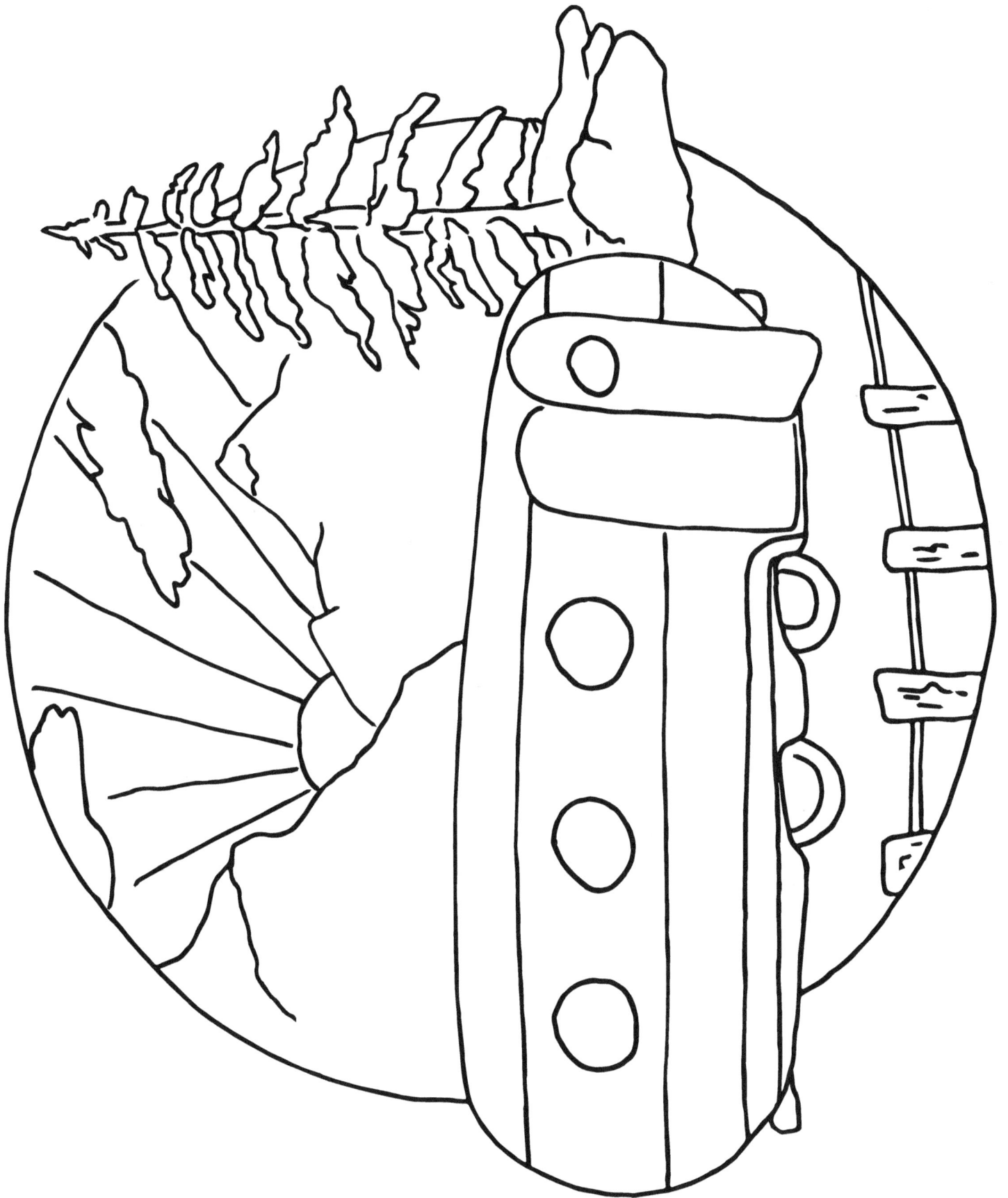

Explore the Pacific Northwest

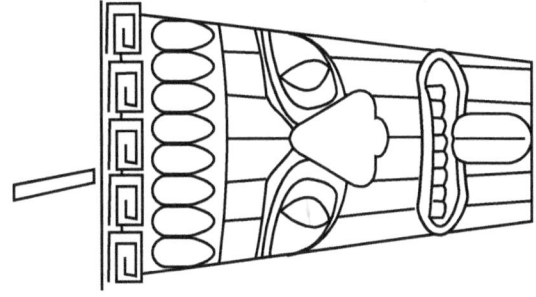

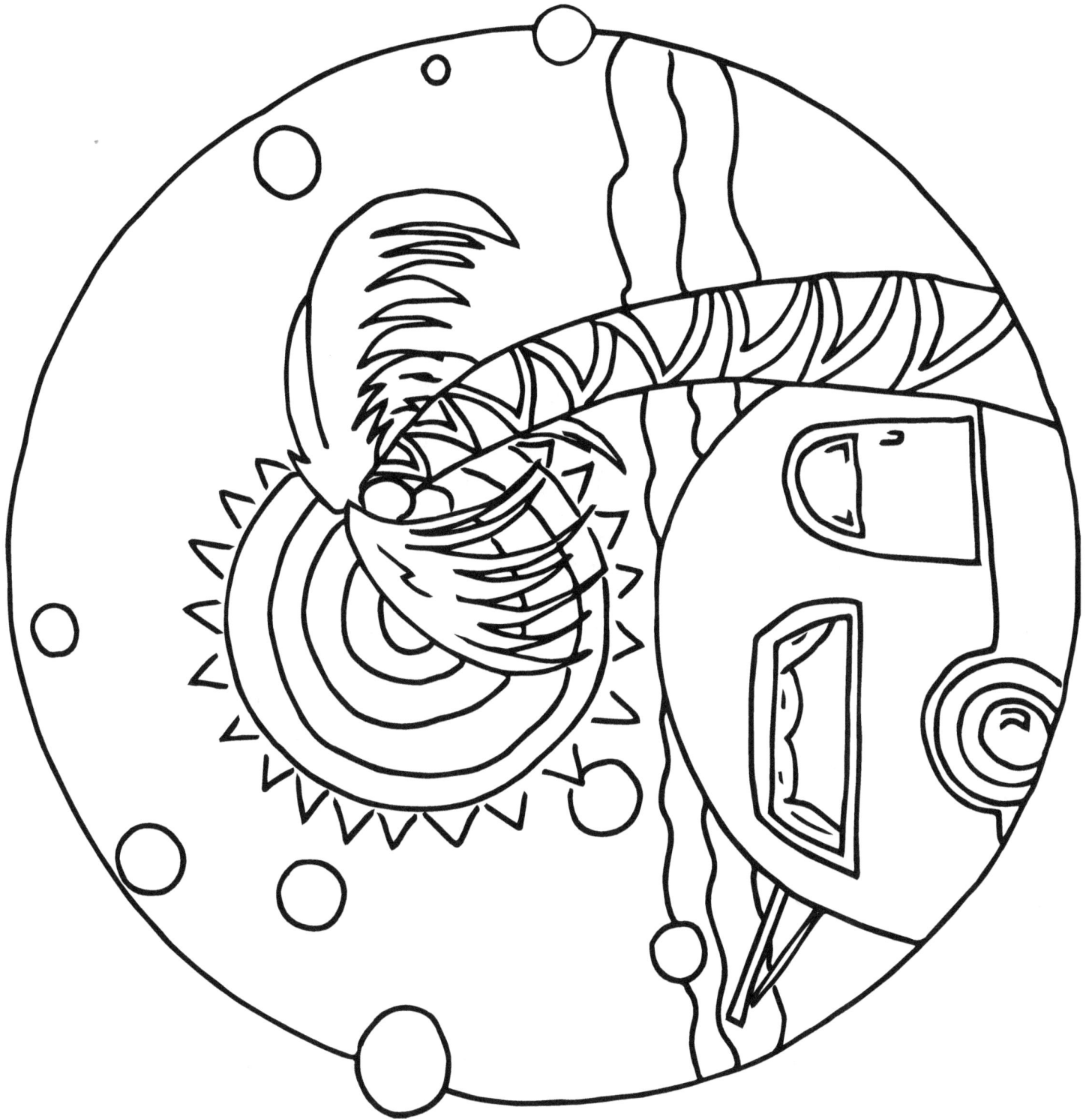

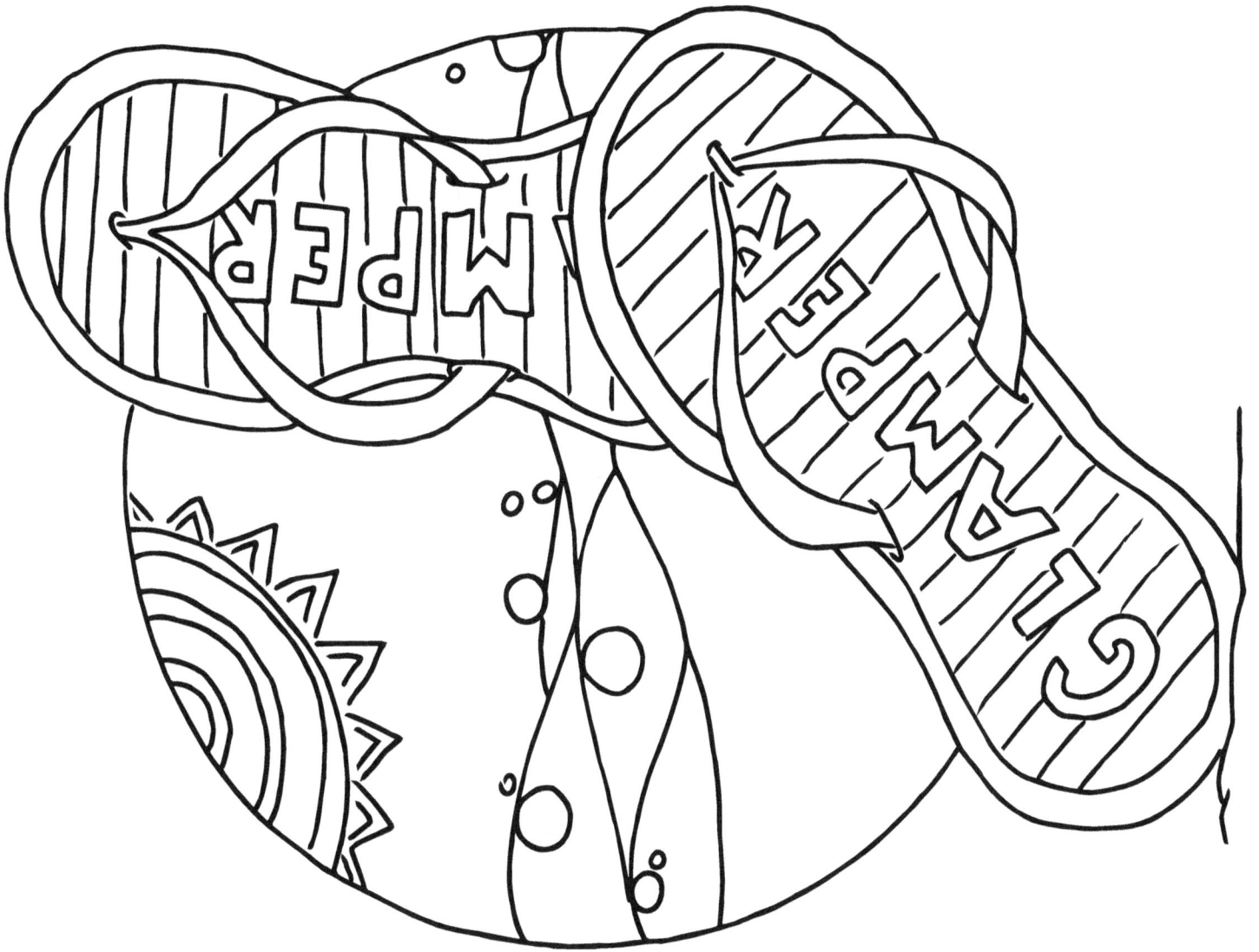

Boondocking GLAMPERS

TIN CAN PURISTS

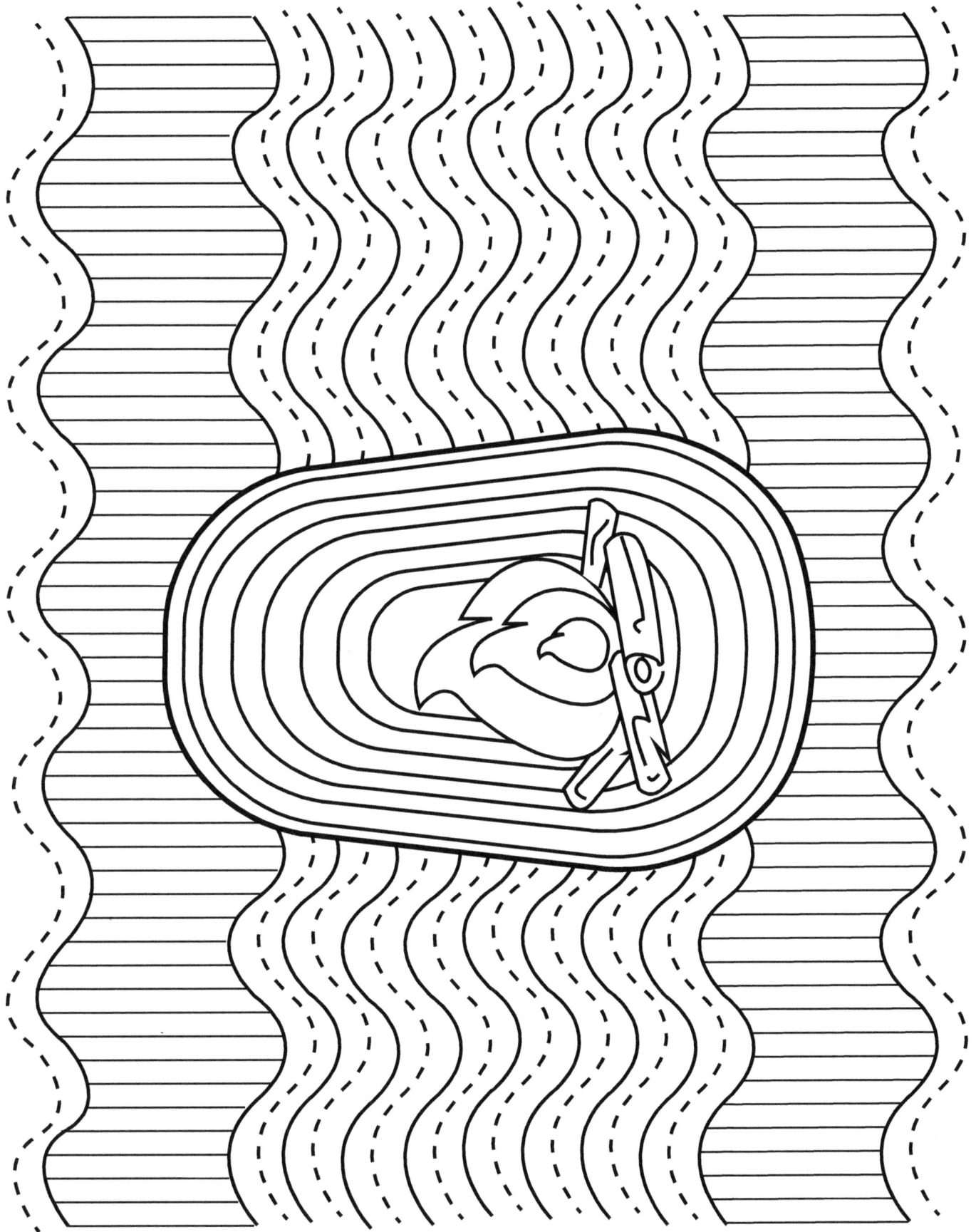

HAPPY GLAMPER

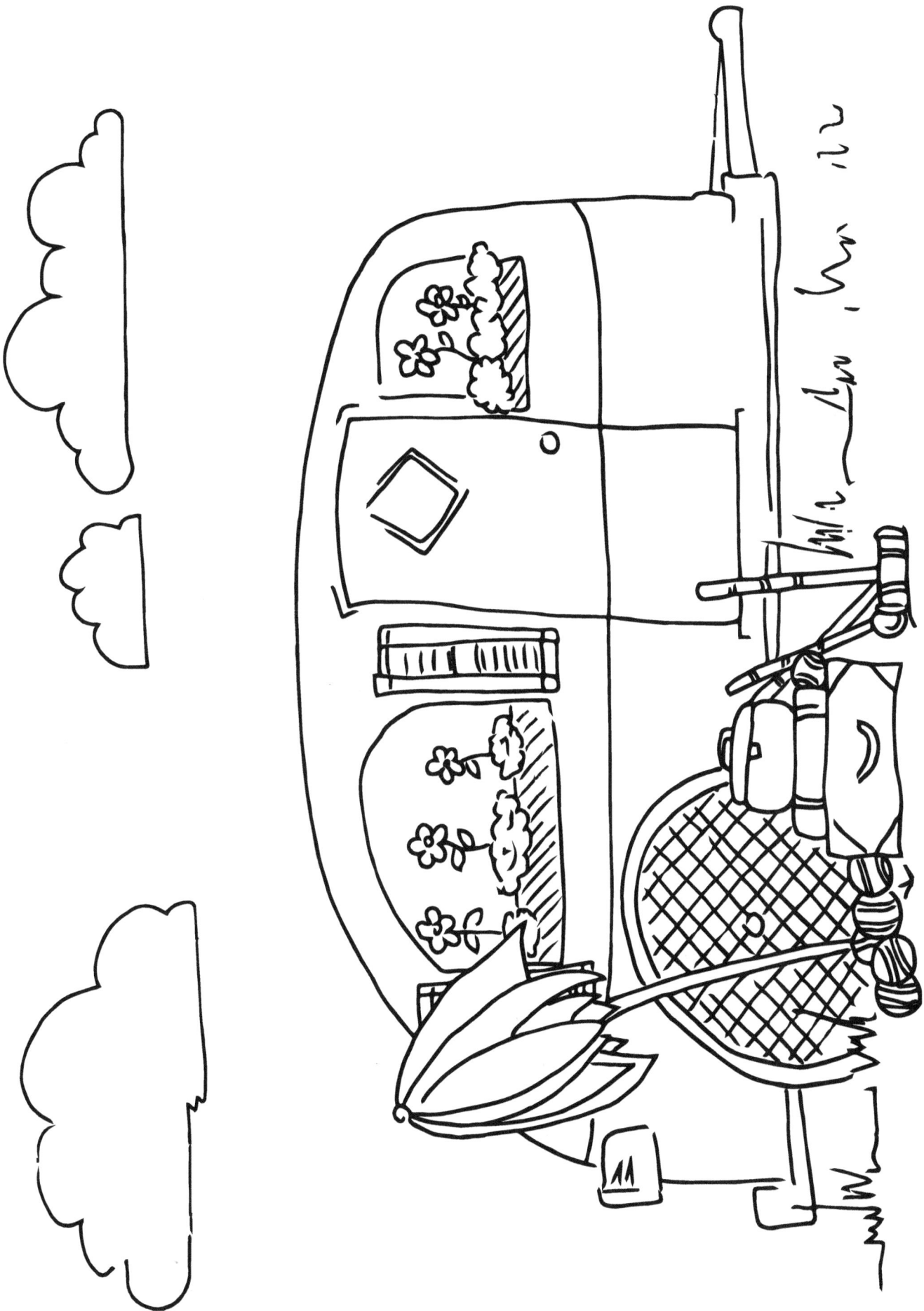

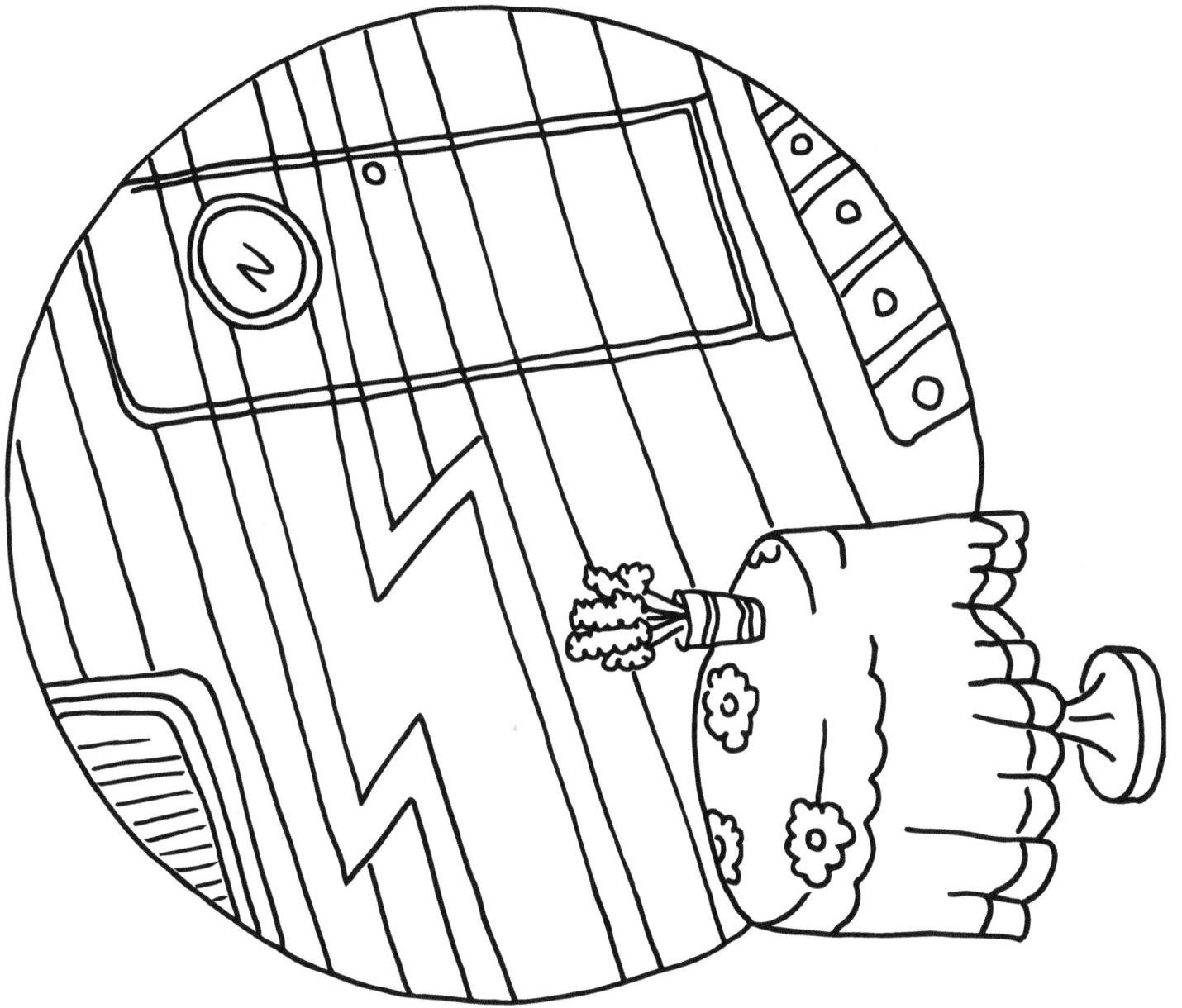

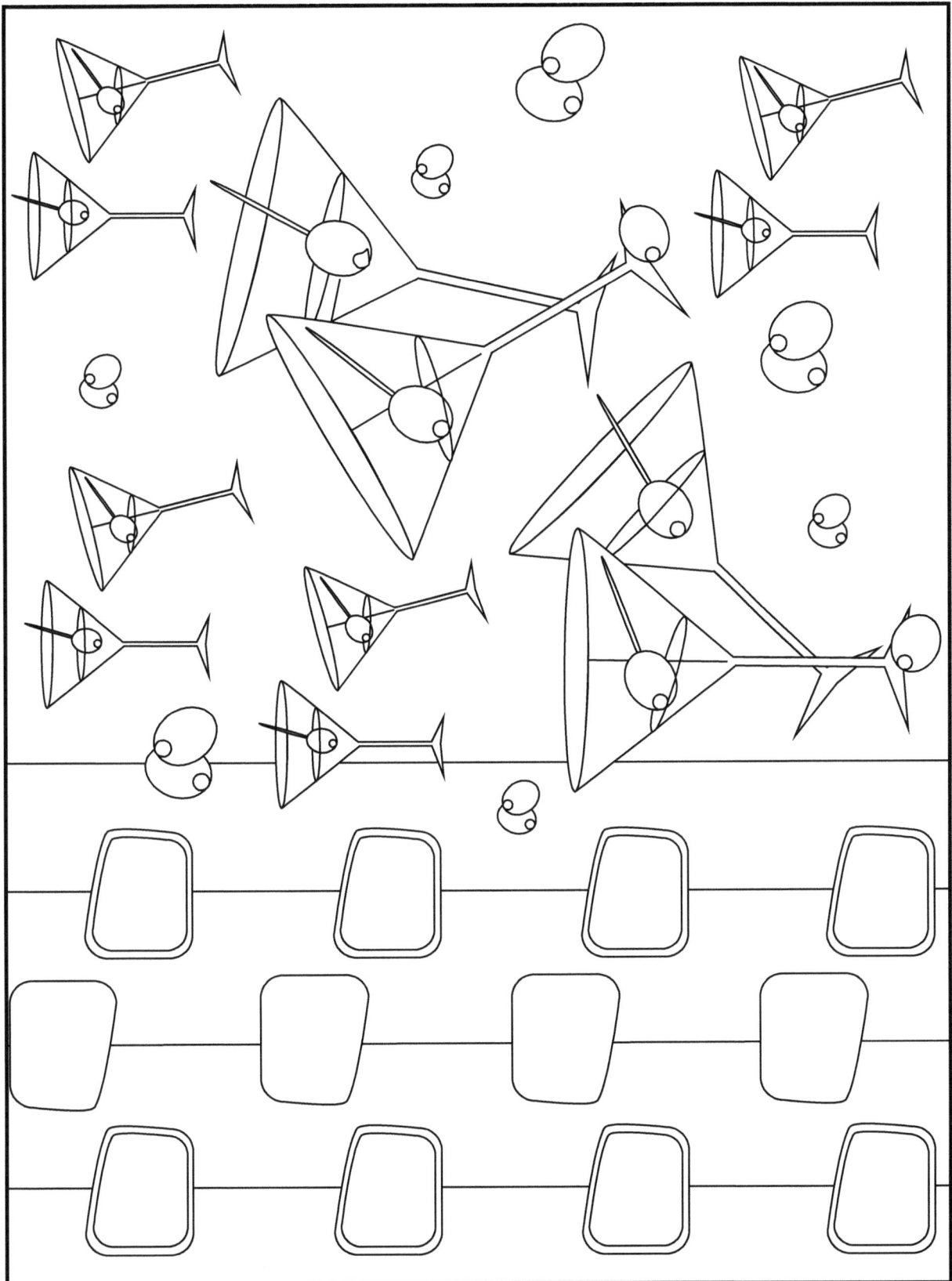

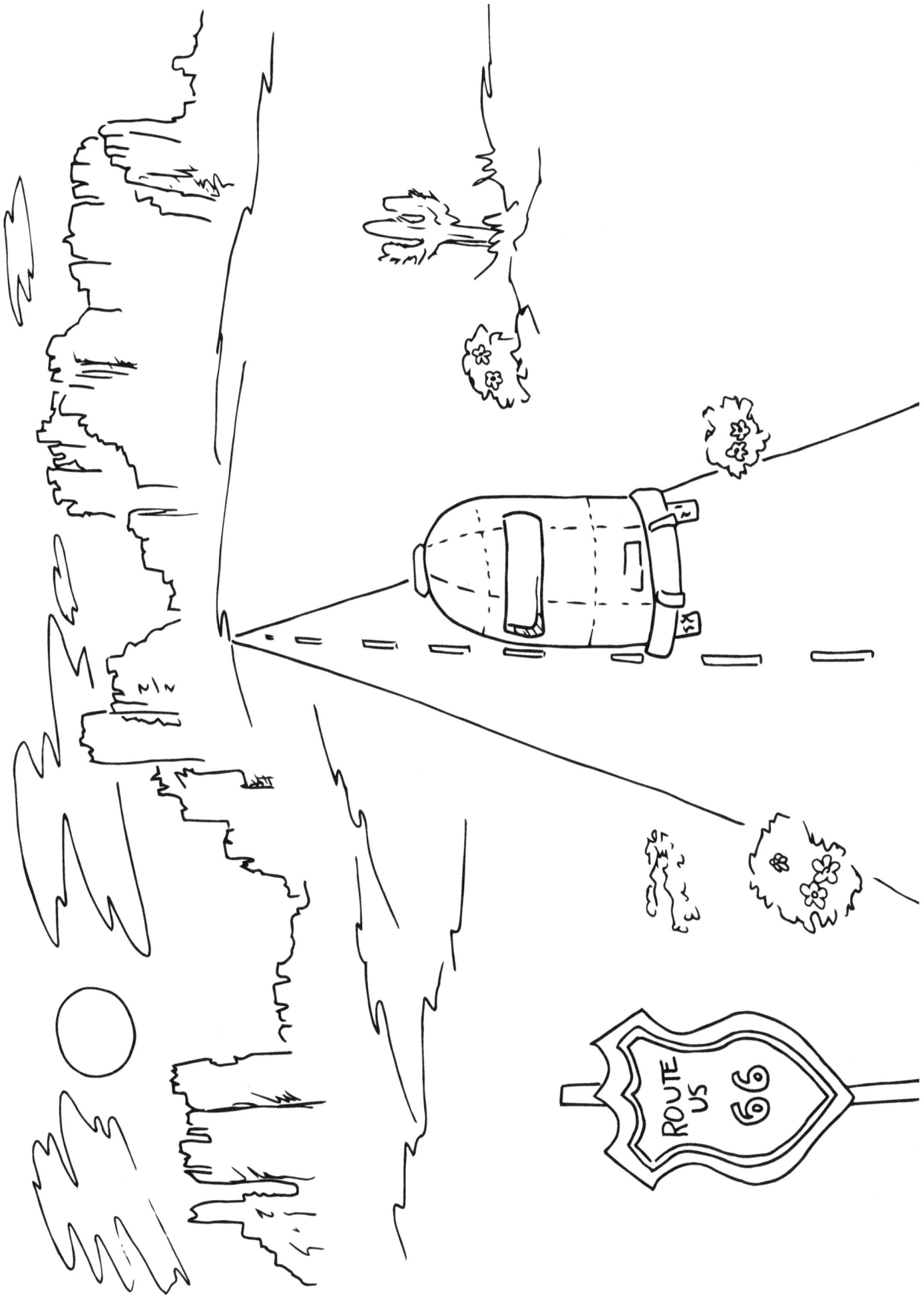

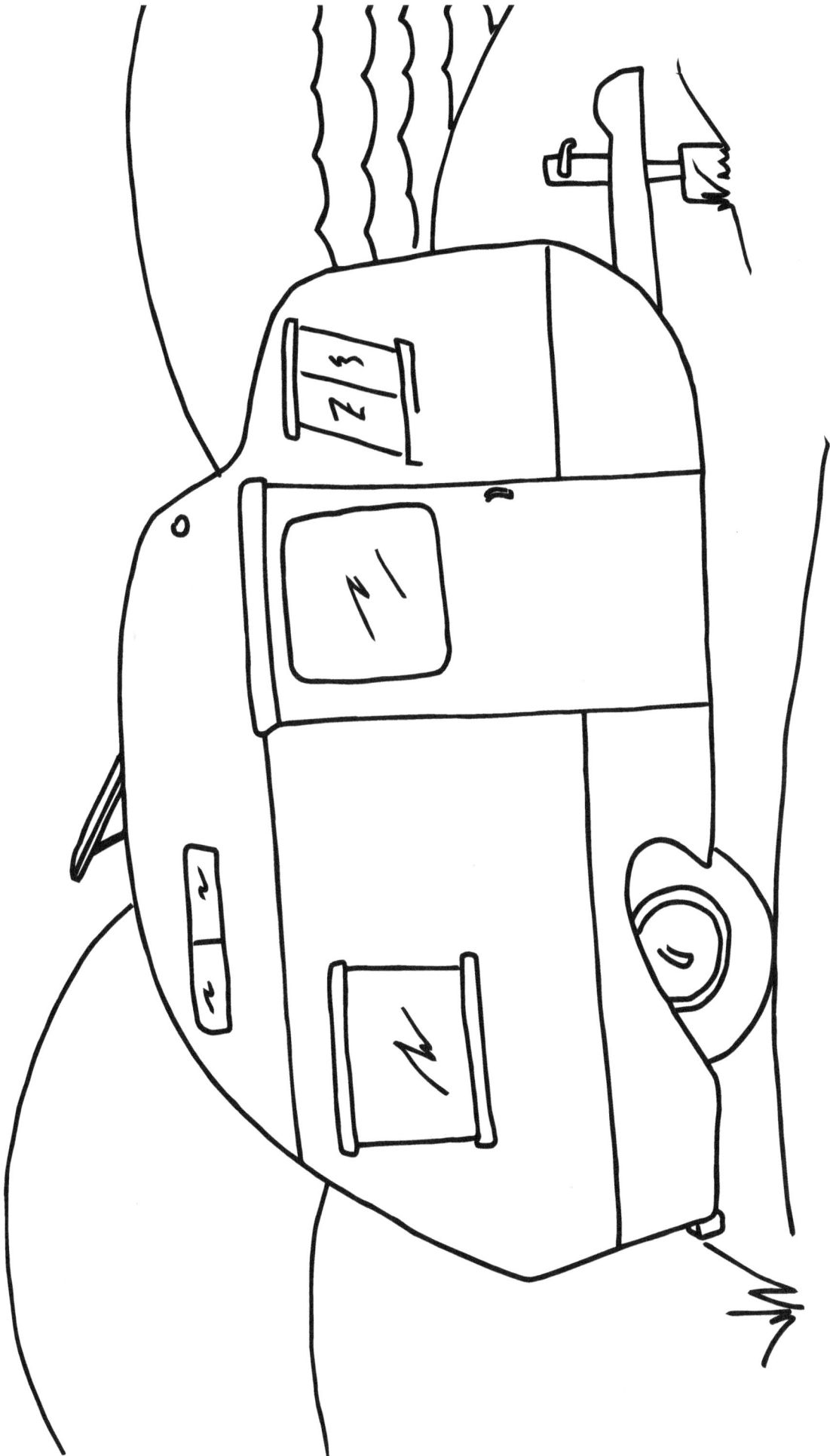

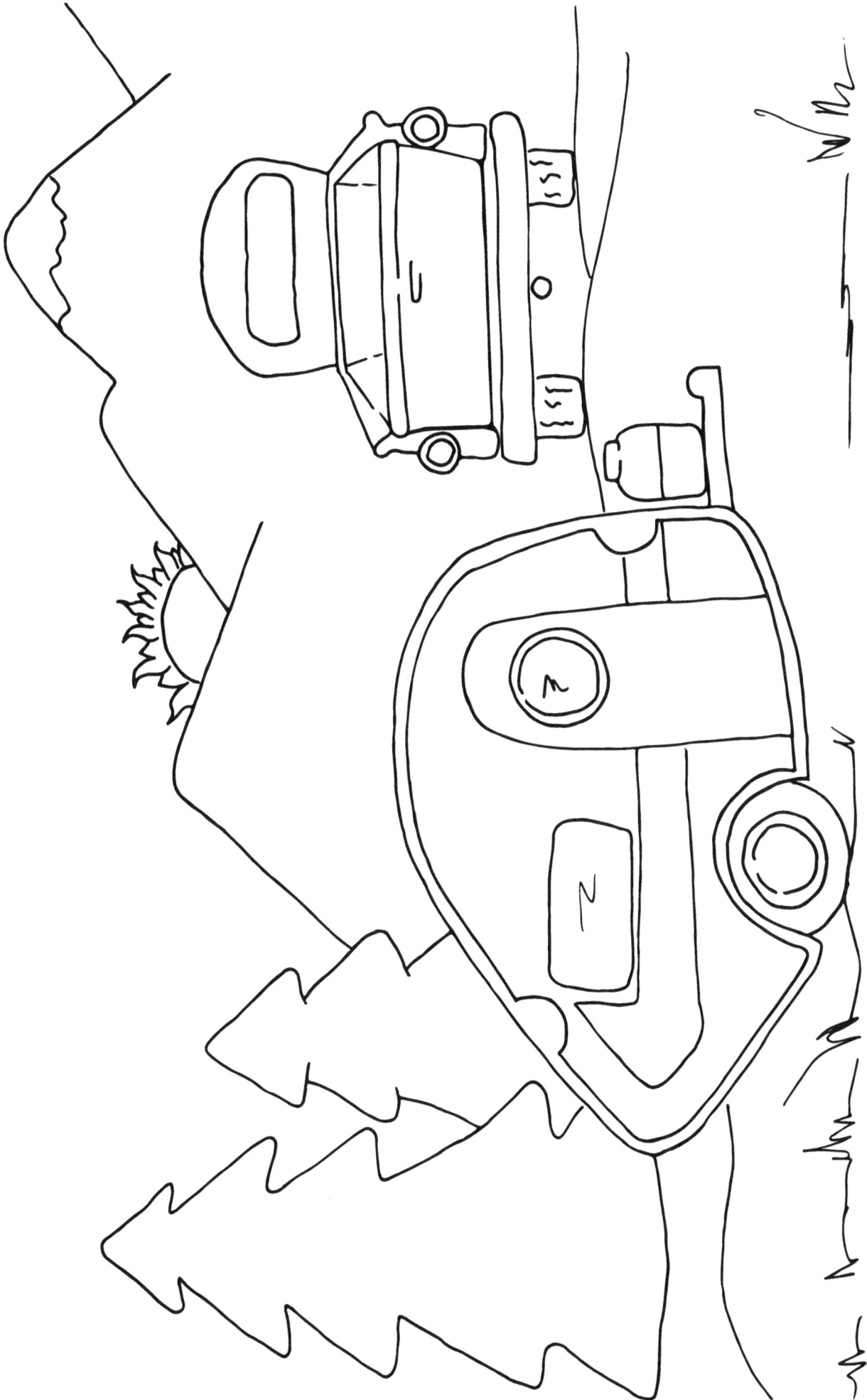

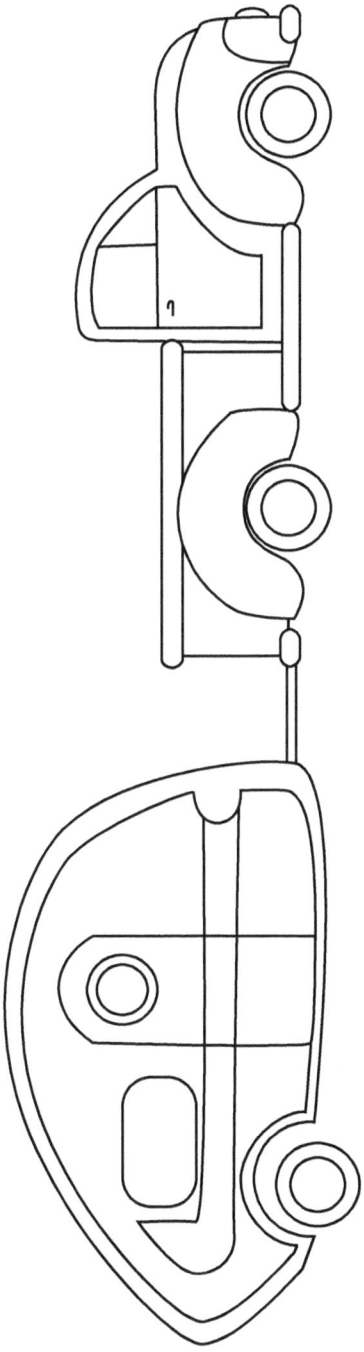

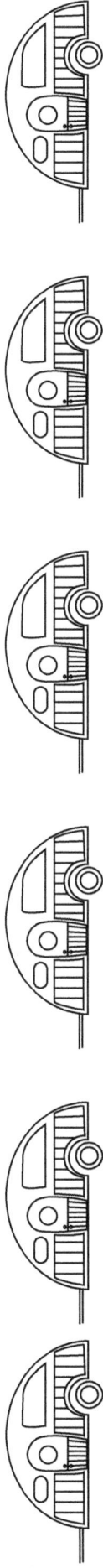

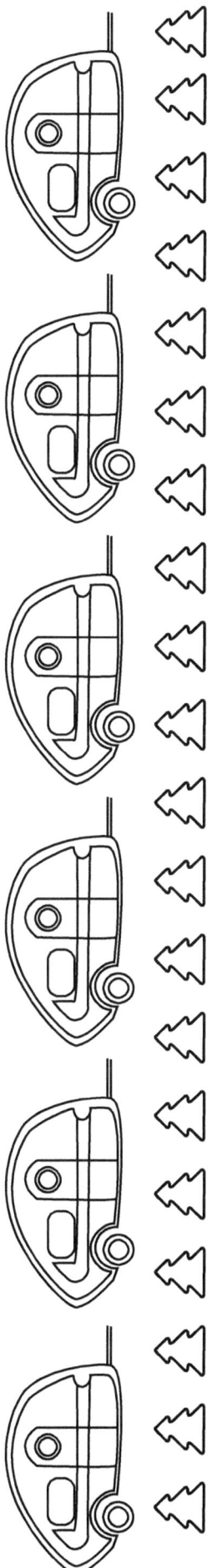

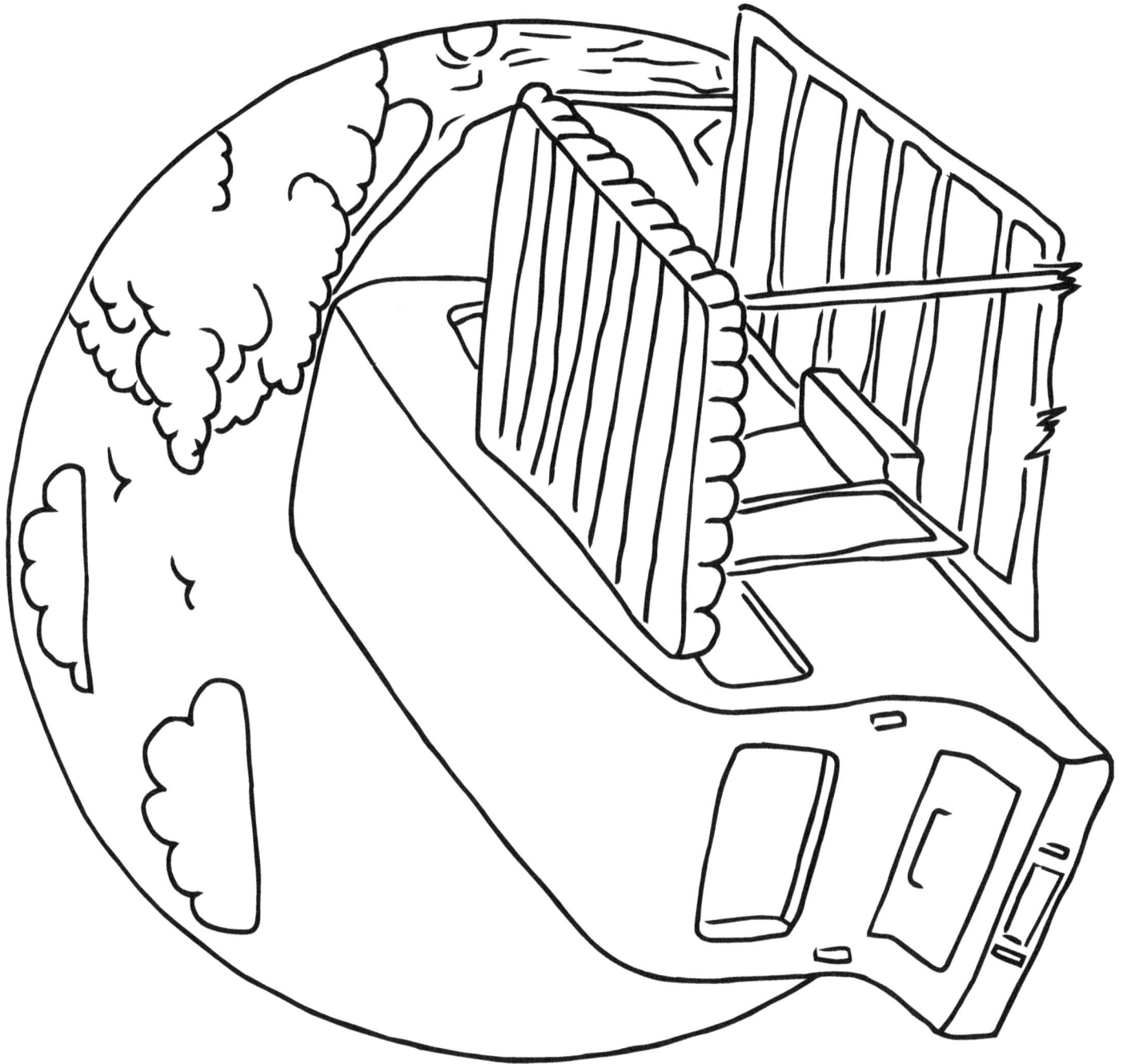

RETRO coloring books .com

Thanks so much for choosing this coloring book.
I hope you enjoyed it! Please connect with me on
Instagram, Twitter, and Facebook by using the
hashtag #retrocoloringbooks. I would love to
see everyone's awesome creativity.

Look for future releases from me on my Amazon page
by clicking follow on my author profile or by going to
the website www.retrocoloringbooks.com.

RETRO
coloring books
.com

www.ingramcontent.com/pod-product-compliance
Lightning Source LLC
Chambersburg PA
CBHW081214020426
42331CB00012B/3028